A 30 Day Supply of Butterbean Parables

By Pat Freeman

Table of Contents

Foreword and References

Pat Freeman shares her heart from a lifetime of faithfully following the Good Shepherd. She has served and continues to serve as an encourager and mentor to so many, I am excited to see her wisdom now put in print form. These devotions will feel like you are sitting down and talking with Pat personally over a cup of coffee. You'll be stirred, challenged, encouraged, but most importantly you will be grateful to read it. ~ Whit Lewis Senior Pastor, Longview Heights Baptist Church, Olive Branch MS, and First Vice President Mississippi Southern Baptist Association.

Pat has a knack for loving people and the gift of an artist. Those combine in this volume. Pat paints pictures with words that speak to the soul. These short reflections and warm remembrances draw the mind heavenward while looking at earthly things. Like a hot soup during a cold winter, they are good for the soul. ~ Dr. David Wyndham, Associate Pastor, Longview Heights Baptist Church, Olive Branch MS

Acknowledgements

Writing a book is like birthing a baby. It has been a long journey to get this, my first one, ready for print. My husband has been my cheering squad. He has listened, endured the hours of silence and given input when asked. Final printing would not happen without him. Thank you to Tracy Crump for your expert professional editing skills. I heard a good writer was a good rewriter. The rewriting has required a lot of self-discipline. My children and grandchildren have given so much input and encouragement. I love you dearly. And then there's Jenni Rust. Just when I was ready to throw in the towel of frustration, Jenni rescued me. She put this book together, the cover design, the formatting and the final touches are awesome. Jenni you are over the top. Thank you so much.

Stinking Thinking

Finally, brethren whatever is true, whatever is honorable, whatever is right, whatever is pure, whatever is lovely, whatever is of good repute, if there is any excellence and if anything is worthy of praise, dwell on these things.
Philippians 4:8

Do you have a tray of rotten eggs in your mind that causes you to have stinking thinking? Each egg is a treasure that represents a wrongdoing someone else imposed upon you. You remember it well! You know the exact day, time, and place, and your mind replays the entire scene, forcing you to experience all the horrible details and emotions related to the event.

A tray of eggs left in your refrigerator would eventually rot and cause everything in the refrigerator to stink. The only solution is to throw the eggs away, wash the tray, and refill it with good eggs. We can do the same thing in our minds. by throwing away the entire tray full of bad memories, retrain our mind, and fill it with good memories. You would not remove those eggs from the garbage and put them back into the refrigerator.

Unexpected words or sights can bring stinking thinking back into our minds. We can choose to dwell upon them, or we can choose to replace them with wholesome thoughts from the Word. When we put our thoughts in light of the knowledge of God, we are better able to put them in their right perspective. Joy and peace are found when are minds are filled with thinking about the good, the lovely, the honorable.

Chose to fill your mind with things that are worthy of praise.

Sleepless Nights

Therefore, encourage one another and build up one another, just as you also are doing. We urge you, brethren, admonish the unruly, encourage the fainthearted, help the weak, be patient with everyone.
1 Thessalonians 5:11, 14

My mind loves to wake me up around three o'clock in the morning and steal my sleep. I can close my eyes, pretend I'm asleep, count my blessings, and make lists, but nothing seems to restore sleep. However, there are times when my lack of sleep is not coincidental. Some nights, God wakes me because He wants undisturbed time with me.

Recently, one early morning, my sleep was interrupted by the presence of the Lord calling me to Him. His glory filled my senses, and I became fully aware of His presence and He had something to say to me. I went to my special place where I meet with God and got down on my knees.

Images of people downloaded into my mind, family members who were sick or struggling and friends caught in the battles of life who needed encouragement. As their images came into my mind's eye, God made me aware of their specific needs and gave me words that would encourage them. I began to take notes so I would not miss anyone when morning came.

God also reminded me that my spiritual gift is exhortation and I should be about my Father's business. The next day, I contacted the people from the list I had made and called to encourage them.

We all need encouragement from time to time. When God speaks a message into your spirit for someone else, be faithful and deliver it.

Put On Your Big Girl Pants

Now gird up your loins like a man.
Job 38:3

If one more person tells me to put on my big girl pants when I just want to complain about how tough life is, I'm going to scream. I really don't want their advice. I just want their sympathy. But I need to hear their words.

Sometimes others can see our problems from a different perspective and convince us that life is really not as bad as we think it is. They shed light into our darkness and encourage us to change. God has a way of sending those outspoken people into our lives to tell us what we would never say to ourselves. As painful as it is to hear those tough words, we know God loves us enough to send a messenger.

When Job complained to God about how tough his life was, God said the same thing my friends tell me but with God language. In Job 38, God told Job to gird up your loins Job, put on your big boy pants——and listen while God instructed him on how He created the world.

God put things in the right perspective for Job. We have to do the same thing when we experience tough situations by putting life in the right perspective. I may not want to hear it any more than Job did, but sometimes I have to put on my big girl pants, and persevere through my tough trials.

Time in God's word helps us keep our trials and tribulations on earth in the right perspective. Although today seems as though it will last forever, this, too, shall pass.

Storms on the Horizon

My first trip to the quilt show in Paducah, KY, took place on a stormy weekend. My friend and I had rented a room in a farm home with a beautiful lake in the back and a long porch across the front.

One late afternoon, I walked to the lake. The smooth clear water changed suddenly when fine drops of rain began to fall. As the farm animals moved to the barn, I stayed to watch the rain. Soon the raindrops became larger and more frequent than I expected, and before I could walk around the lake to return to the house, the gentle rain had turned into a large frightening storm.

The following night, it stormed again but this storm did not make a gentle approach. We were sitting on the front porch and the first indication of a storm was the sound of the hanging ferns hitting the porch ceiling.

The storms that attack our lives are just as diverse. Some come in like a gentle rain and reap chaos while others slap us in the face like ferns hitting a ceiling.

The storms will come but no matter the intensity of a storm or the effect upon our lives, we have a shelter, and His name is Jesus. He is always with us. Leslie Gould once said, "Sometimes God calms the storm, but sometimes God lets the storm rage and calms His child."

Jesus is always there with outstretched arms. Don't let the storms of life get you down.

The Shadow of the Cross

The two little boys stood at the top of the hill and then laughingly rolled over and over all the way to the bottom. Covered with grass and heads wet with sweat, they climbed to the top for another trip. The pasture that ran beside the expressway was one of their favorite places to play. They leaned against a post for a short rest before their last trip down. One of the boys pointed down the hill. "Look, there's a shadow of a cross going down the hillside. Where did it come from?" Looking up, they realized the post they were leaning against was the base for a man-made cross. They were playing in the shadow of a cross.

We live in the shadow of a cross every day. We live, work, and play in the shadow of the cross that Jesus placed in our lives more than two thousand years ago. The old rugged cross that provided our salvation still casts a shadow so big it covers all our sins and shame.

When we roll down the hills of life and are covered with trials and tribulations, we can lean against that cross for rest and forgiveness. It stands through time and eternity, straight, strong, and empty. It is just as empty as the cross the little boys were leaning against in the pasture. Jesus has ascended to heaven where He sits at the right hand of the Heavenly Father to intercede for us.
That cross makes the difference for us.

Don't Let the Geese Get You Down

Then when lust hath conceived, it brings forth sin; and sin, when it is finished, brings forth death.
James 1:15

Canadian Geese covered the church parking lot They were so comfortable in the lot that cars had to maneuver around them to get into parking spaces. Then, we had to make the precarious walk through the lot to miss all the residue they left on the ground.

When the geese first took up residence in this area, we thought they were curiously interesting. But as time has passed, they have multiplied. In addition to the undesirable excretions they leave in the most inconvenient places, the geese have no fear of humans, and obnoxiously and unyieldingly walk in areas we are trying to occupy.

Sin is like that when it moves into our lives, sometimes as quietly as the geese did. At first, we are attracted to sin. We make excuses. We learn how to maneuver ourselves close without becoming a part of it. We convince ourselves that we are just looking until one day we become fully engaged in the sin. That is exactly what Satan wants us to think. Just as the geese have made our southern land their home, we have allowed sin to take up residence in our lives. We have to identify sin for what it is and run from it.

An idiom from the past is still true today:

"Sin will take you further than you want to go, keep you longer than you want to stay, and cost you more than you want to pay." ~Ravi Zaccharias

Seasons of Life

Do not fear, for I am with you; do not anxiously look about you;
for I am your God. I will strengthen you, surely, I will help you,
surely, I will uphold you with My righteous 'right hand.'
Isaiah 41:10

In the fall, some of the trees in my yard quickly become void of their leaves. They stand naked and alone, braced for the coming winter season. But the trees only appear to be naked and alone. The unseen expansion of their root system is preparing them for the coming spring season when they will need extra strength to withstand the winds and rains.

Sometimes we experience a fall season in our lives when we feel naked and alone; everything that could go wrong, goes wrong. Through those tough times God reminds us that He is with us. We have no fear, we do not anxiously look about. We are like the trees putting down roots. God calls us into a growing season that allows our roots to grow deeper in His Word to prepare us for a coming season of difficult times. He is our God and our strength comes from Him. He waits for us to call upon His name and He will hold us up with His righteous 'right hand.' Spending time alone in His presence is our root growing time when He is helping us to understand His will, He is strengthening us for the season ahead when the storms will come.

The fall seasons of life are not to make us fearful and anxious, they are seasons for putting deeper roots into His Word.

God Keeps Notes

My four-year-old daughter stood on a stool and stirred the cake mix and then she poured the mix into cupcake tins. With a little help, she got the cupcakes into the oven. Soon they were ready, the tea was poured, and she and her brother were off to her room for a tea party.

Her father and I quietly stood at the door watching and listening to our children talking about what good parents they thought we were and how lucky they were to live with us. They loved the country life and all their domestic pets as well as the barnyard animals. The sweetest words a parent ever hears is that their children are happy with what has been done for them.

Our heavenly Father has the same desire to hear His children bragging about how happy we are with what He has provided for us. He listens to us just as intently as we listened to our children. His heart is glad when He hears us speak His name to others. Every time He hears us speak of Him, He writes a reminder in His book. It is exciting to think there is a library in heaven full of books filled with everything we have said on earth about God.

I look forward to spending a day with my Lord and listening to Him read a book to me about every time I talked about Him while I was here on earth. What a day that will be.

The Edible Word of God

*Your words were found and I ate them, and your words became for
me a joy and the delight of my heart; for I have been called by
Your name, O Lord God of hosts*
Jeremiah 15:16

The year 2005 was one of the most challenging years of our marriage. My husband had a coronary bypass surgery and carpal tunnel surgery on both hands. I had spinal cord surgery that left me in a very weakened state. Heartache after heartache piled upon us until one night we said enough!

We packed our bags and ran away from home. The car became a cocoon for us to see exactly where we were in life. Running away did not solve all our problems, but it gave us a new perspective. One night, we were in Asheville, NC, and I became so distraught, I had to stop and seek God's counsel from His Word. I isolated myself and turned to the book of Jeremiah. Jeremiah, the weeping prophet, gave me words of consolation, wisdom, and encouragement over and over as I sat and read for hours and poured my heart out to God.

Our omniscient God knew me before I was born and knew that on that day, I would need those exact words. Like me, Jeremiah was so hungry for God he was ready to eat the scrolls before him. I was so hungry for God I could have torn pages from the Bible and eaten them. God, met me at my point of need and gave me peace. He always meets us when we seek His face.

There is not a problem so big God cannot solve it.

Quit Trying

I can do all things through Christ who strengthens me.
Philippians 4:13

When I was a child and my father told me to do something, he wanted it done, and he wanted it done swiftly. When he asked me about my progress, I would tell him I was trying to get it done. His response was always, "Well, quit trying and get it done."

Have you ever been told to quit trying? Trying to do something is an excuse for not completing a project. The definition for the word trying is "exerting strength or attempting." I have a list of things I try to do, but they never get done.

Time to throw that word trying away and replace it with doing what needs to be done. Doing is a work in progress. When we choose to do all things as unto the Lord, without fussing and complaining, we accomplish what has been set before us.

Today, I am doing that closet organization I have been trying to get done for some time, or I'm cleaning the garage, or I am straightening that room I have shut the door on. Keep your list short so you won't get overwhelmed. Do all you can each day. When I approach my chores, I always begin with my least favorite and complete that one first. The best time to get that dreaded job done is before you do anything else.

We strive to live like Jesus and his world is in perfect order. Perfection is unattainable but keeping our lives in order is possible.

Let the Heavens Rumble

In my Father's house are many mansions; if it were not so, I would have told you. I go to prepare a place for you. And if I go to prepare a place for you, I will come again, and receive you unto Myself; that where I am, there you may be also.
John 14:2-3

The heavens are noisy. Thunder is loud enough to make the house shake, and lightning crashes all around, but I'm not afraid. Instead of fear my imagination goes into orbit every time a storm arrives.

I try to decide if the angels are moving furniture around. Or maybe they are having a bowling party? I love thinking the angels are working on my mansion. They could be adding stones to my rock garden or building me a fountain on each side of the entrance. Perhaps they are even enlarging the patio beside the swimming pool. It could be a new mansion going up on the other side of the lake in front of mine. I really like the thought of a neighbor.

When we accept Jesus as our Savior, we become children of the King. He begins preparing that mansion in heaven he promised us. He says there will be many mansions and one day He will return and take us home to be His neighbor and live in a mansion close to Him. Jesus loves us so much He wants us to live eternally close to Him. This could be the dawning of that grand and glorious day.

Let the heavens rumble. Maybe today the building will stop, and Jesus will come for His children.

Alarming Headlines

Woe to those who call evil good, and good evil; who substitute darkness for light, and light for darkness, who substitute bitter for sweet, and sweet for bitter.
Isaiah 5:20

Every day, depravity and corruption are paraded in front of us by the news media, social media, or daily conversation. Sin is paraded with arrogance. No one confesses to wrongdoings, no one is condemned or held accountable. Our leaders flaunt their crimes and laugh in our faces. What is lawfully wrong seems to be right for some, while others are punished for the same thing. The darkness of sin becomes overwhelming.

Do the headlines in the news media alarm you? Sexual immorality has become so common place that it seems to have taken away the need for young men and women to marry. Young people go through a stage in life of searching for who they are and now they are being told to question their own gender. Sweet has been replaced with bitterness.

When is this going to change, we ask? More and more, we are beginning to choke on the moral decay swiftly moving in upon us. We are having to protect our righteous ground like never before. God's Word speaks specifically to the changes we are witnessing today, but evil will not always reign. Every day we long for our Lord to return and take us home to be with Him. Take heart, dear Christians. 2 Timothy reminds us there is a crown of righteousness which the Lord, the righteous Judge, will award to all who have longed for His appearing.

I have a longing in my heart for Christ's appearing. He will make all things right again. Are you ready for His return?

Sharecroppers

You are the light of the world. A city on a hill cannot be hidden.
Matthew 5:14

Sharecroppers do not own land. They work the land that belongs to someone else and they give half the profits to the landowner as pay for the privilege of living in whatever house is available. My father was a sharecropper. We usually had to live in run down, dilapidated derelict shacks.

We did not have electricity or running water in the first house I remember. After our few belongings were moved in, my brothers and I rambled through looking for what might have been left behind by the previous occupants. In a drawer in the kitchen we found some candles and matches. We sat on the floor and melted the candle tallow allowing it to stick our fingers together. Soon the candles were burned down. Then the night came. We had misused the light during the day with no knowledge of the darkness of night and the fear it would bring.

Today we are no more than sharecroppers living in the wonderful world Jesus has provided for us. We have the light of the gospel in our homes, and we are misusing it, just like children playing with the only candles in the house. God's Word is the light of the world, even though almost every home has a Bible in it, many of those Bibles are never read nor are the Words in them shared. We are misusing the gospel if we are not sharing.

Be encouraged to read His Word and share the light of that Word to a lost and dying world. The darkness is coming.

Thy Word is a lamp unto my feet and a light unto my path.

The Mud Puddle

Brilliant blue eyes, full of mischief, were the only recognizable trait I saw from the mud-covered face of my four-year-old son. How could one little boy take a small mud puddle and cover his entire body in dark brown mud and smell so foul? He thought it was the best thing he had done all day, but all I saw was my precious little boy covered in too much mud to come into the house.

An outside water hose and good scrubbing soon removed all the mud from hair to toes. He was clean and smelled much better. He was once again allowed to go into his home.

Jesus has the same response when He sees His children covered in the sins of the world. With just one small weakness in our resistance, we allow sin to creep in and cover us with the mud of the world. Our sin-covered lives are a foul odor and it is time to present our dirty, sin-covered bodies to Jesus and let His precious blood flow over us. He will cleanse us with gentle hands that loosen the toughest stain sin has put upon our lives. Jesus will not stop His cleansing process until we are cleansed all the way to the source of our sins. Only then do we return to God the sweet aroma of His presence in our lives.

Have you been to Jesus for His cleansing power? Are you washed in the blood of the Lamb?

Learning to Lean

Trust in the Lord with all your heart, and lean not on your own understanding.
Proverbs 3:5

In the fall, some of the trees in my yard quickly become void of their leaves. They stand naked and alone, braced for the coming season. But the trees only appear to be naked and alone.

The unseen expansion of their root system, is preparing them for the coming spring season when they will need extra strength to withstand the winds and rains.

Sometimes we experience a fall season in our lives when we feel naked and alone, void of friends, uncomfortable in a situation. Through those tough times God reminds us that He is with us. We have no fear, we do not anxiously look about. We are like the trees putting down roots. God calls us into a growing season that allows our roots to grow deeper in His Word to prepare us for a coming season of difficult times. He is our God and our strength comes from His. He waits for us to call upon His name and He will hold us up with His righteous right hand. Spending time alone in His presence is our root growing time when He is helping us to understand His will, He is strengthening us for the season ahead when the storms will come.

The fall season of life are not to make us fearful and anxious. They are seasons for putting deeper roots into His Word and learning to lean on the strength of Jesus.

Stand in the Blessing Line

He who is generous will be blessed, for he gives some of his food to the poor.
Proverbs 22:9

The poverty of my childhood still influences decisions I make today. My husband and I love to share God's blessings to us with others. We give, not because we have much, but because we know how it feels to have little.

There seems to be an abundance of needy people. Deciding where to donate is important. We begin by looking at the needs of our immediate family. Single mothers struggling to provide for children get high priority, working couples who have lost jobs need assistance, working families with insufficient funds are a good place to target for donations.

God's Word encourages us over and over to give and by our own generosity we are standing in the Blessing Line. Acts 20:25 It is more blessed to give than to receive. My favorite scripture is Luke 6:38 Give and it will be given to you. They will pour into your lap a good measure---pressed down, shaken together, and running over. For by your standard of measure it will be measured to you in return.

We are amazed at how God blesses us because of our own generosity. People bring gifts to our door that are unexpected and unsolicited. They are gifts from the hand of God because we have given to others. Not always are the gifts from someone we have given to but are gifts from others who are obeying His Word.

Stand in God's Blessing Line by giving to someone who is needy today.

Milk, Sugar and Toast

*Jesus said to them, "I am the bread of life; he who comes to Me
will not hunger, and he who believes in Me will never thirst."*
John 6:35

When I first married, I was amazed that we always had food in our kitchen. Plentiful amounts of food, was not something I had in my childhood home. Our drinking water was from a rusty well. I learned to laugh about having to blow the skim of rust off the top of our water, but I have never been able to erase the memory of being hungry or laugh about it. Hunger was my driving force for getting a job following high school graduation.

After I married, I would sometimes go to the refrigerator or pantry and just look at the variety of food we were blessed to have. My favorite foods were milk with sugar and toast, together. I would eat them for any meal or in between for snacks. My taste for food has expanded tremendously, but I still love my milk, sugar, and toast.

This reminds me of when we first accept Jesus. The goodness of the Lord is so sweet we cannot get enough of Him, and the longer we serve Him, the sweeter He grows. I have never forgotten the day I gave my life to Jesus and tasted the bread of God. The bread of God is that which comes down from heaven and gives life to the world. His promise to me that I will never be hungry again goes beyond food. That promise is my eternal security.

His storehouse is full, and He never runs out. "O taste and see that the Lord is good. How blessed is the one who takes refuge in Him" Psalms 34;8

Who Let the Cat Out?

A friend loves at all times.
Proverbs 17:17

The year I graduated from high school, I was given a choice that had never been offered before: I could chop cotton or get married. Guess what I chose? Sixty years later, I am still married to the wonderful person who gave me that choice. He took me straight from the cotton patch to downtown Memphis. It was like letting a cat out of the bag.

We rented an apartment in midtown, and I rode a bus downtown to work. The sights, sounds, people, opportunities, and fun available to me were beyond this country girl's comprehension.

One of the first people I made friends with was the daughter of front-page socialites in Memphis. Her parents owned the company where I worked, but she treated me as an equal. Her "shoe room" was as big as my childhood bedroom. She called my five-and-dime-store dishes china and spoke as though they were as good as her Lenox tableware. Her friendship made me realize I was lovable and she taught me to love others just as I was loved.

One of the most valuable gifts we ever give to someone is our love. Investing ourselves in others is like fluffing pillows around their hearts. Love allows others to develop into who they are. Love is not just something we give away; love is a boomerang that returns in greater proportions than it is sent. God filled our hearts with an unlimited supply. The more love we give, the more love he pours into our hearts.

Who are you pouring your life into today?

What Measure Is Love

For He whom God has sent speaks the words of God, for He gives the Spirit without measure.
John 3:34

By what measure is love? Sometimes in worship we sing a song that speaks of our Father's love being too great to measure. The dictionary defines measure as a way of determining extent. We measure something almost every day, either in some form or other. God programmed calculations into our brains when He created us. Revelation 21:17 tells us even angels use the same measure as man: "And he measured its wall, seventy-two yards, according to human measurements, which are also angelic measurements."

But God does not use the same measurements that humans and angels do. He has his own set of measurements that go far beyond our comprehension. We cannot measure the pain He felt when He gave His only Son, Jesus, to the world as a gift, to provide for our redemption. How do you measure the self-control God possessed to turn His face from His son, Jesus, and allow man to crucify Him?

When Jesus fed, he fed in abundance beyond measure. When He healed, He overwhelmed. When He taught, it lasted for hours and was captured for eternity. And when He loved, oh, how He loved.

He loved enough to reach from time past to time future, to cover everyone who chooses to kneel at His cross and be washed in His blood. God's love gave us His Son who was willing to bleed every drop of His own blood that we might have life eternal. That is love without measure.

Have you experienced His limitless love?

The Pony in the Kitchen

Therefore, the redeemed of the Lord shall return and come with singing unto Zion, and everlasting joy will be upon their heads.
Isaiah 35:10

The laughter from the kitchen was not just excessive, it was explosive. My momma alarm rang louder when the children grew silent at my approach. Never did I expect to see Roscoe, our Shetland pony, standing in the middle of my kitchen being fed from the refrigerator by my daughter.

A pony can be led up the stairs, but you cannot force him to go down the stairs. Roscoe activated every contrary trait a Shetland pony possesses. It took us hours to remove a frightened stubborn pony from the kitchen, but we managed—and without any damage to cabinets or floors. Roscoe was as happy to return to his barn stall as we were to see him back where he belonged. A Shetland pony does not belong in a kitchen.

Have you ever been the pony in the kitchen? Suddenly, you are in a situation you never expected to be in. Friends have convinced you to come along for the ride, promising you don't have to get involved. But there you are eating, drinking, doing drugs, or engaging in some sexual situation you never planned. Or maybe you are just watching as other participate in immorality. That is not where God created you to live. Christians sometimes find themselves to be the pony in the kitchen.

A bad decision can side track us but does not have to identify us. It can be overcome with a Christ centered session with appropriate counselors.

Bad decisions do not have to determine destiny. Make the decision to walk away from what is taking you down.

The Yellow Fog

Rescue the weak and needy; deliver them out of the hand of the wicked.
Psalm 82:4

One of our favorite places to fish is the White River in Arkansas. In the late afternoons when the sun drops low in the sky, the warm summer air above the cooler river will sometimes create a thick, yellow fog. Seasoned boaters know that as soon as the atmosphere creates that eerie yellow, it is time to get off the river. We sit on our dock and watch the river become alive with happy voices as they pass. Only their silhouettes are visible through the fog.

Occasionally, a newcomer to the river will either be unaware of the conditions or fail to heed the change of color and become lost in the fog. We can hear the fear in their voices as they flounder through unfamiliar waters looking for the river channel.

Their frightened calls for help are soon answered by seasoned boaters, who tie ropes to the lost boats and pull them to the docks and safety. Cries of fear soon become joyful sounds of wellbeing.

What a humbling picture. We hear the cries of those floundering in sin, lost in the fog, because they are unfamiliar with the channel Jesus has already provided. We cannot remain bystanders. As Christians we have to rescue the perishing. Some Christians on the banks of the river stand in prayer for those who are in the channel of the river rescuing souls

Rescuers must be willing to go into the deep waters of the lost and mentor them, making a personal connection to their lives and leading them to Jesus.

You Gotta Cross That Bridge

Then you will walk in your way securely and your foot will not stumble.
Proverbs 3:23

One of the scariest things I have ever done was walk across the swinging bridge over Royal Gorge in Colorado. I bravely started the trip across, but in the middle, I looked down and realized I was way out of my comfort zone; I became paralyzed with fear. All I could see was 955 feet of space to the dirty river below me. I had to move across that bridge in one direction or the other.

Life is like walking across a swinging bridge that has a lot of unknown space we have to muddle through. Don't try to walk it alone. Spend time in prayer with God. He promises in James 1:5 that if we lack wisdom, we can ask Him and He will give it to us in abundance.

If we stop and look down at all our circumstances, we may become paralyzed with the enormity and not be able to function. We have to decide what is the right direction for us and trust God to get us over that bridge. Once a decision is made, don't rethink it. Trust yourself to have made the right decision at the time, under the circumstances. Cross that bridge and move on with life.

We have a Savior that will hold our hand and walk with us all the way across those difficult, frightening bridges. God has set a path before us, and we must choose to look ahead and walk in it.

Our God never leaves us or forsakes us. That promise is good for every bridge we cross.

The Leader of the Band

*Be imitators of God, as beloved children; and walk in love, as
Christ also has loved us and has given Himself for us an offering
and a sacrifice to God as a fragrant aroma.*
Ephesians 5:1

Every day I watch the teenager walk to the bus stop. The walk is part of the waking up process—slumped forward with clothes that look frumpy and unkempt, disheveled hair, eyes only partially opened. I fear for the stumble that might cause a fall on the uneven sidewalk. The heavy back pack would surely take him to the ground.

He survives his day looking forward to his last class. Music is his world and band the last class. He suddenly comes alive and is the first person on the field with his baton in hand. Every fiber of his being is alive as he waits for the band to take its place. He is no longer in a daze for now he is the leader of the band.

What a comparative description of the lives of many Christians today, stumbling through life, unaware of anything but what is right in front of them. They do not take time in prayer and God's Word to prepare for the day, so the slightest upset throws them to the ground. Yet they are looking forward to heaven and the promises God made on the day of salvation.

The most important goal in our lives is a future in heaven. Time to stop stumbling around and just surviving. Prepare yourself for the cracks in the sidewalks of life and don't get thrown by them. There is victory in Jesus.

Time to wake up and walk worthy of His calling.

Lights in the Sky

Then Jesus again spoke to them, saying, "I am the Light of the world; he who follows Me will not walk in the darkness, but will have the Light of life."
John 8:12

Walking the boardwalks in Orange Beach, Alabama, is exhausting. I retired early to bed one night, only to find that, despite my exhaustive state, my body still only required six hours of sleep. I quietly slipped out and onto the deck of the condo in the early morning darkness. While I waited for the sunrise, I spent my time thanking God for all the blessings He pours out on me.

Dark clouds insinuated approaching heavy rain. The only visible color was the white caps of the water in response to the high winds. Soon, the black clouds were joined by a glimmer of red. Then color burst into the blackness and crawled around the edges of the gulf waters. God's amazing artwork began to unfold as the water slowly began to reflect all the colors from the sky.

With the enormous color palette God owns, I can only imagine how He will decorate His sky when He sends His Son Jesus back to collect His children. But with all that beauty, I know His children will not be looking at the sky but at the face of their Savior.

Our lives are like that morning sky, dark and colorless until we let Jesus into our hearts. The moment we accept Him, our lives begin to shine with color, and the more we live for Jesus, the more colorful and vibrant our lives become.

Formula for the Fountain of Life

The fear of the Lord is the fountain of life, that one may avoid the snares of death.
Proverbs 14:37

Realizing how swiftly the senior years of my life are passing has forced me to come to terms with my own immortality. I find myself looking for products that will make me feel better, look younger, and have more energy. My time here on earth is shorter than it has ever been. God numbered my days, but He did not share that number with me. Is there a way I can extend my days?

I have found the formula for the fountain of life. It is located in a very old book I keep in my home. It is the book that has the answers to all my problems, all my questions, and all my needs. This book, the Bible, also gives me guaranteed assurance of living longer if I do exactly as it says. The Bible gives me the formula for the fountain of life. I must fear the Lord.

My fear of the Lord is a wholesome fear of knowing who He is and who I am in Him. My Lord not only saved me from an eternal death to an eternal life, but He promises wonderful benefits in this world also. Fearing the Lord allows us to obtain wisdom, knowledge, prolonged life, confidence, refuge, contentment, humility, freedom from envy, and the comfort of the Holy Spirit. He has promised all this and more to those who abide by His Word.

We have the assurance that Jesus will do what He says He will do.

Wheels Just Keep on Rolling

*Truly, truly, I say to you, when you were younger, you used to gird
yourself and walk wherever you wished; but when you grow old,
you will stretch out your hands and someone else will gird you,
and bring you where you do not wish to go.*
John 21:18

I'm so blessed I don't have to walk everywhere I go. Today I have wheels and I love them, especially if they are moving down a runway, expressway, or highway. They are taking me someplace different than where I am. I have been fortunate enough to have covered a lot of territory in my lifetime.

But the aging process has slowed my travel considerably and I know it will eventually stop. The only wheels I utilize now are the ones on my car which carries me a lot of places.

Life on this earth does not last forever and I have to enjoy as much of it as possible. Decisions determine my destiny and I decided to serve the Lord in every location my wheels have carried me.

Once, while in Sioux Falls, South Dakota, I prayed with a grandmother as she sat at the falls grieving for a grandson that had overdosed on drugs. In Hawaii, I cried with a woman whose husband had left her for her best friend. On an airplane, I shared Jesus with a young man that had never heard the name of Jesus. I realize my days on earth are getting shorter and I will not always be in control of where I go and what I do, but today I will live for Him.

Wheels can take us many places but the name of Jesus is appropriate to share in any location.

Mully Grubs

I was so overwhelmed by darkness I couldn't face the day. I wanted to go to my room, shut the door, and cry to the wind. Everything I had allowed to become an offense rumbled through my mind like a tornado. I wanted to spend the rest of my life locked in a dark room, living in the mully grubs. I did not need anyone, no one loved me; I was totally unlovable.

Even in my distress, I kept remembering something my favorite counselor told me years ago. "If Satan can isolate you, he can destroy you." I had to make myself get up, get out of the house, and go to Bible study.

During the lesson, my teacher looked me straight in the eye and said, "Do not nurse offenses. Do not rehearse wrongs done in the past." How did she know that message was for me? I had allowed my mind to become the victim of vain speculations and lofty thinking. It was knee time, time to break the stronghold in my mind that held me captive. I needed to retrain my mind by taking every thought captive. No one else could do that for me.

God was waiting for me to come to Him, and He met me there that morning. I left the Bible study without the dark cloud I had taken in. Somewhere in my time with God, He had removed my darkness and filled me with the light of His Word.

Do not nurse offenses or wrongs, done to you in the past.

Light at the End of the Tunnel

The mind of man plans his way, but the Lord directs His steps.
Proverbs 16:9

My husband and I had so much fun on Christmas Eve when our children were young. We stayed up all night assembling toys and talking of how they would love what we had purchased for them. Morning brought the squeals of delight that made all our sleepless hours worthwhile.

The year we bought our son an electric train for Christmas became a very memorable year. It was such fun, watching the father-and-son interaction as they lay in the floor together playing for hours. My husband had a favorite route for the train that took it out of town, up to the top of a mountain and then down a fast pass back into town. My son loved the trip around the lake, through a long dark tunnel and back into town. His favorite part was watching for the light as the train came out of the dark tunnel

It was comical to watch our son wait until his father had set up the track for his mountain pass, and when the train went through the switch station, our son would switch the tracks and take the train around his favorite route instead.

Many times, we make plans to take the high road to the mountain top and then whiz down the steep path on the other side, screaming with glee. But we cannot always whiz down the mountain tops and the fast passes. Sometimes God chooses to take us through the dark tunnel, the deep valley, and the shadows of death to teach us that, in every dark situation, He has directed our paths. He is the light at the end of every tunnel.

Whichever track we choose in life we can be assured our God is directing our paths.

Unconditional Love

Beloved, if God so loved us, we ought also to love one another.
1 John 4:11

She knew how to work a crowd. With her head held high, blue eyes twinkling and a smile that spread from ear to ear, she captivated the entire room. As she walked across the floor, she made eye contact with each person for a second, giggled, shrugged her shoulders, and then directed her charm to the next person. When someone responded to her, she moved into their arms, surrounding that person with the biggest, warmest hugs she could muster and planting warm kisses on their cheeks.

It never occurred to her that someone would not love her. No sense of hate or malice existed in her heart. She didn't know what a grudge was nor how to hold one. Love flowed through this six-year-old Down syndrome girl into the arms and hearts of everyone she encountered; an unconditional love that knew no boundaries. Her ability to not see race, social status, emotional disharmony, or prejudice captured the room, and for a few moments, the entire room was in harmony.

God calls us to that same unconditional love that knows no boundaries, does not see race, social status, prejudice and no emotional disharmony. Jesus displayed unconditional love when He walked this earth Himself. When God sent His Son Jesus to earth, He personally delivered a perfect love package. There is no greater love.

We love because He first loved us.

Call Me

*Now we who are strong ought to bear the weaknesses of those
without strength and not just please ourselves.*
Romans 15:1

I spent my childhood in the country and would not date country boys because I wanted to live in the city. My husband grew up in the suburbs and I had no idea his dream was to live in the country.

After nine years of listening to him beg to move, I finally gave in and moved to the country. It was a very traumatic move for me. One day, home alone and walking the floor totally embroiled in a full- fledged pity party, one of my city friends called. "The Lord laid you on my heart, and I just wanted to tell you I loved you." I burst into tears, glad to have someone to share my misery with. My sweet friend just listened. Then she told me something I didn't want to hear. The apostle Paul had learned to be content in whatsoever circumstance he was in. Her words did not comfort me. "That was before God made Mississippi," I cried.

How wonderful to have a friend that responded when God placed me on her mind. I learned a lesson that day. When God places someone on my mind I will respond and contact them. That person may be suffering or in a desperate situation, and God wants to use me to answer her cry. Satan would never tell me to call a friend in distress.

I am strong today, but tomorrow I may be the weak one and need your strength to help me through my day. Call me.

Biography

Pat Freeman writes and teaches Bible Studies in her home, in conjunction with her church. She uses life situations combined with scripture to encourage others. Difficult situations in her life and four near death experiences have brought her into a deeper walk with the Lord. She has a unique understanding of how temporary life is and how important it is to depend upon the Lord for guidance. Pat was featured in a world-renowned spine clinic because she survived a rarely successful spinal cord surgery.

She has been published by Guidepost and is featured in a book by Mary Alice Kenley. She writes devotions and shares them regularly on social media. She also wrote devotions for her previous church for their monthly newsletter.

Pat pours her life into younger women, teaching them that Jesus and His Word is the answer to the situations they encounter in this life.

You can reach Pat by email at butterbeanparables@gmail.com.

Made in the USA
Columbia, SC
23 August 2024

41036286R00024